Magical Mac
The True Story of a Healing Horse

To Mary Ellen,
Who knows
~~this~~ Magic
intimately!
Love,
Michele
and
Alexandra

April 2006

Acknowledgements and Dedications

*To all McDougall's friends, our supportive friends, and those who enhanced this book:
Amanda, Anastasia, Andrea, Carol, Claudia, Harold, Joanne, Judith, Kay, Kevin, Klea,
Leslie, Linda, Maggie, Marian, Mary Anne, Megan, Michele, Mom, Nick, Rebecca,
Randa, Sally, Space, Stephanie, Stuart, Tom and the Horse-Sitter.*

*We lovingly dedicate this humble tome to all of Mac's friends—past, present and future.
We recognize and appreciate the "magic" which flows between all of us.*

MICHELE

And to Adi Da Samraj, my Spiritual Teacher, who Happily Blesses everyone
and everything—the 2-legged, 4-legged, many-legged and no-legged.

ALEXANDRA

© copyright, Michele S. Davis, Alexandra Makris, 2002

Photograph of Avatar Adi Da Samraj with horse © 2002 The Da Love-Ananda Samrajya Pty Ltd,
as trustee for The Da Love-Ananda Samrajya. All rights reserved. Perpetual copyright claimed.
Used by permission of the copyright owner.

Cover and book design by Crowfoot Design

Magical Mac
The True Story of a Healing Horse

By Michele S. Davis, Ph.D. and Alexandra Makris, M.A.

McDougall's Gift of Magic

BY CLAUDIA TEATSORTH

~The Magic Is Great ~The Love Is True ~The Heart Is Pure ~The Power Is Healing~
Healing Is a Gift ~The Gift Is Wellness ~The Wellness Is the Legacy~
~The Legacy Lives On~

Let your heart believe in McDougall's gift to heal and the magic of love.
Let the children have hope, for hope can bring magic to life.

Claudia is an avid animal advocate and has rescued many cats, dogs and horses along the way.
She has been actively involved with the Serendipity Stables' healing horses and
attended McDougall's 50th birthday party and his memorial service.

Mac's Farm—Serendipity Stables

McDougall ("Mac" for short) always had a reputation for honesty. Before his arrival at Serendipity Stables in York Center, Ohio, Mac was a school horse. He was known as a good baby-sitter because the youngest, most inexperienced child would receive the best possible riding lesson from this dependable old gelding.

This is the story of Mac—
A great horse, not just any old hack.
You'll hear it told
That he valued like gold
All young children who sat on his back.

"Hello, may I introduce myself?"

Old McDougall was his name,
And bright healing grew his fame.
He did it with great pride,
Taking all in stride.
For Mac's caring touch, children came.

By word of mouth, Mac's reputation for being gentle with children grew. He was safe for children to pet and groom—and they could even sit on his back.

Loving children played out back
With McDougall—without tack!
To them it was quite clear:
He was a horse very dear.
So they named him "Magical Mac"!

Throughout his long life, Mac had many names. Affectionately called "Big Mac" or "Old Mac," McDougall captured everyone's attention. Because of his black-and-white tail, he was known as "Skunk." He was also known as "Mr. Tie and Tails" and "Whispering Winds." The children who loved him took his naming one step further.

Mac's beautiful black-and-white tail
Was full blown, like an ocean boat sail.
And with grizzled old face,
Aged, but with grace,
Old Mac remained hearty and hale!

Old Mac flicks his tail

When Michele bought McDougall, she was led to believe that he was seventeen years old. Actually, he was thirty years old! He had the constitution of a much younger horse, even though signs of aging were apparent.

Mac and Michele
(Do you see how much they love each other?)

So wonderfully black
Was Old Magical Mac . . .
Four white legs and pink lip
(The cutest bit of pink snip!)
And a white crescent moon on his back.

Mac's favorite manure pile where he loved to play and nap!

ost horses do not have McDougall's amazing coloration.
ow many horses have you seen who are black with a
hite tail? Not to mention that he sported four white
ockings. This unusual pattern made it easy to trace
s history. Mac was black-and-white because he was
ecially bred to stand out in a parade!

Through his eyes deep and bright
Flowed wisdom and light.
His sure step and sharp ears
Belied his great years
Like his 17 hands of horse height.

Old Mac ruled Michele with an iron hoof. As a fantastic teacher and a determined boss, this gentle giant (a thoroughbred and saddlebred mix) totally changed the path of her life. But that is another story!

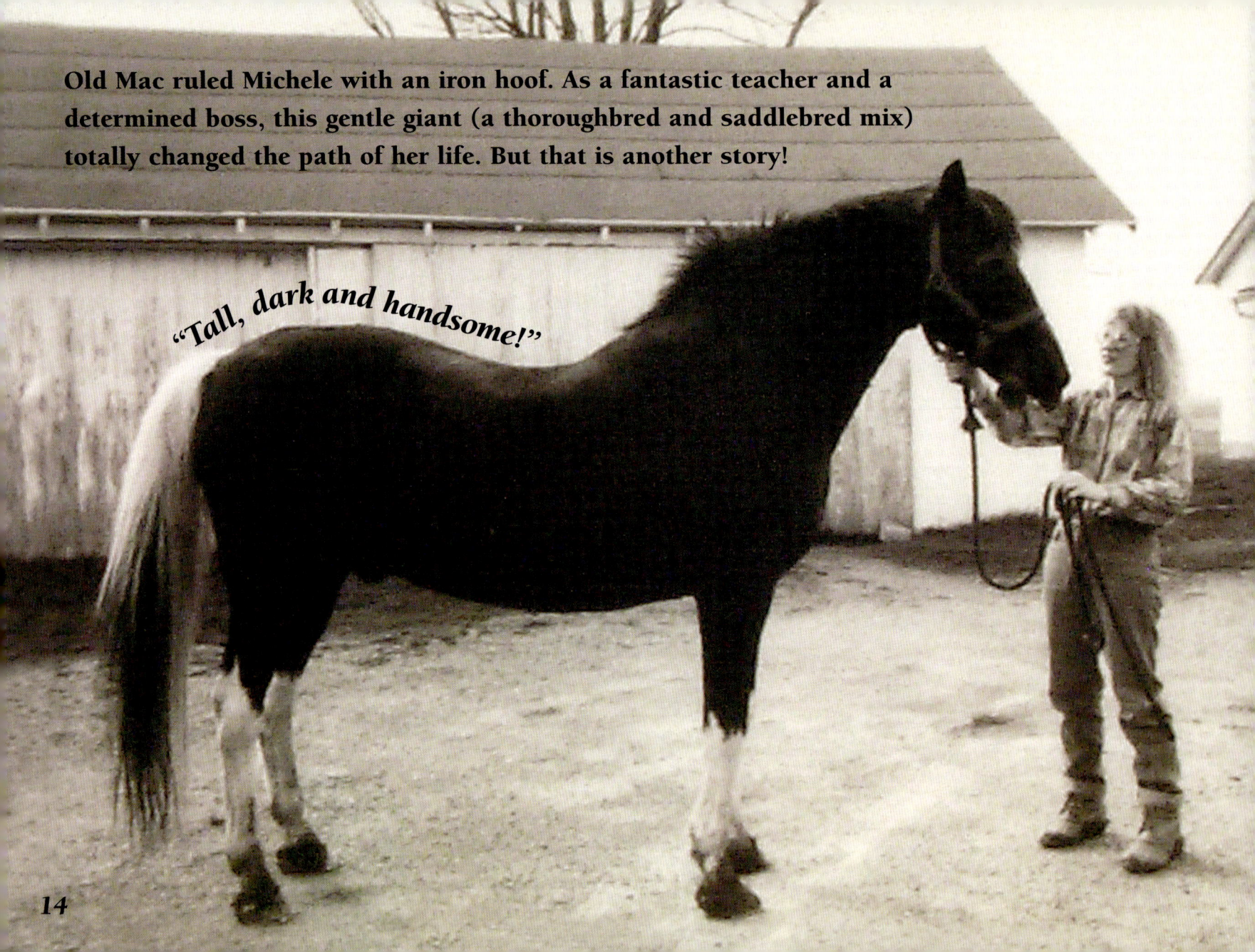

"Tall, dark and handsome!"

From horse work Old Mac retired,
And for magical work soon was hired.
Such was the case,
That he found a new place
In the world, as a healer inspired.

McDougall had done it all. He excelled as a jumper, but also performed dressage (fancy movements like horse ballet). He was an accomplished parade horse and also did well as a trail horse and, of course, as a school horse. McDougall accepted his new and inspired work with enthusiasm and determination.

McDougall with two-legged friends

McDougall's first noted healing was an autistic boy who was speechless and withdrawn. While his parents looked on, the boy lay stiff on Mac's back. Then his rigid fingers twitched and he made a strange noise. He was trying to pet and speak to Mac. McDougall had begun to heal him!

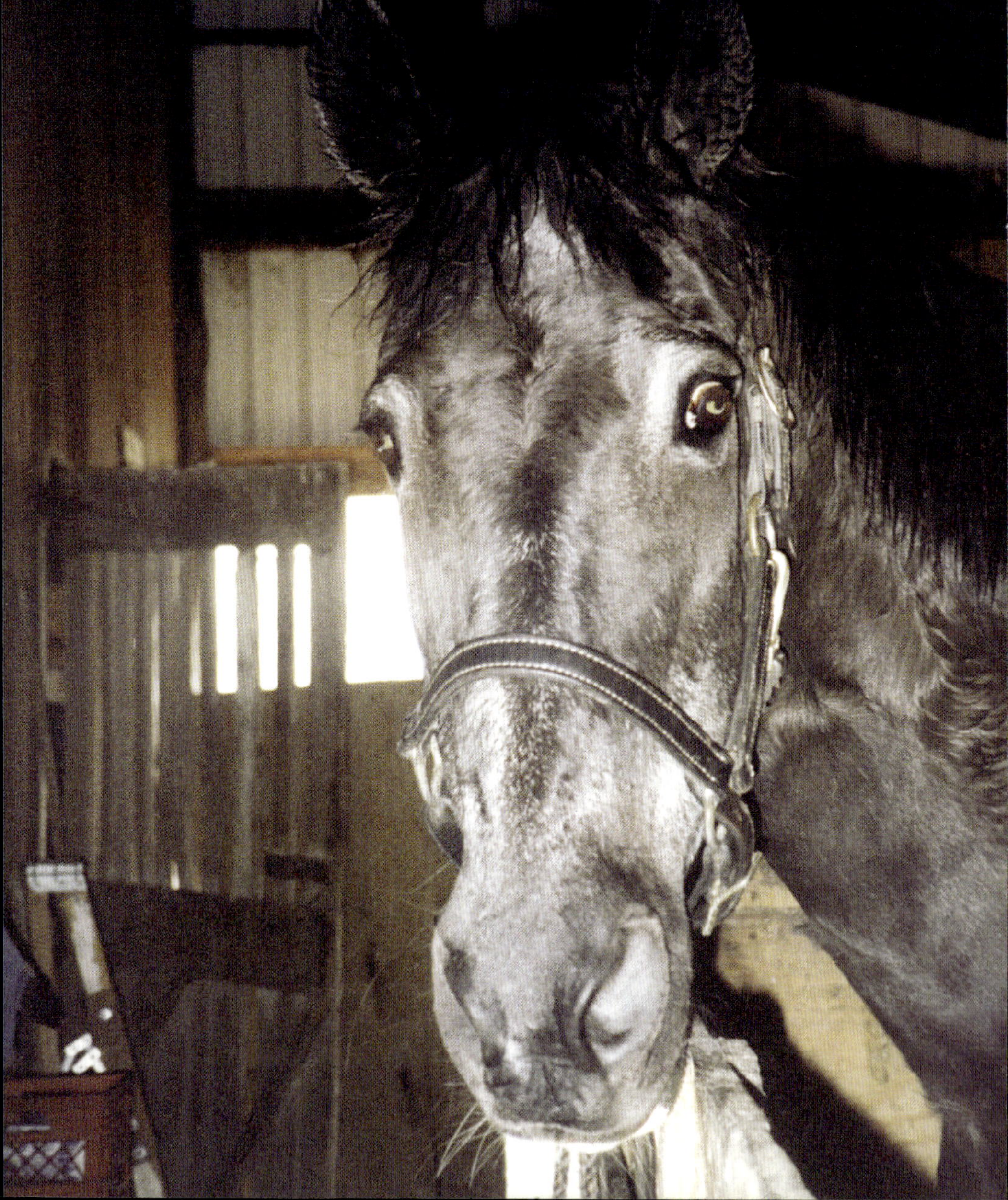

As children in need came to his side,
Old Mac would give them a ride,
Or he'd stand still and tall
Doing nothing at all,
Just shining bright from deep down inside!

Mac is happy to see Gabby

Initially, families brought their children to the farm with the intent of having them interact with a safe horse. To everyone's amazement, the gifts of Magical Mac proved far more valuable than could have been imagined.

"I feel tingly all over!"

McDougall would stand very still when he was healing a child. Often his eyes would take on a faraway gaze or he would close them. He usually breathed slowly and deeply. Once he finished his healing work, he would stroll calmly around the barnyard with the child on his back.

A great equine healer and friend
To the children he wanted to tend,
Mac worked hard as he could
To do immense good,
Putting many sweet babes on the mend.

Caring parents, who had exhausted the traditional means for healing their children, would find their way to Serendipity Stables in search of hope and health in the form of an old black horse.

When Sammy first visited McDougall, he was very pale and thin. Regular sessions with Old Mac gradually changed Sammy's condition.

"Look at me, Mom."

Sammy was a tiny guy,
He could not eat and was so shy.
Mac took command
With an equine helping hand
And Sammy felt better by and by!

"This feels good!"

Emily, sweet little kid,
Couldn't sit still—she just did what she did.
She needed some calm,
Some good healing balm.
That she got when on Mac's back she slid.

Emily was often hyperactive and loud. It was exciting to watch her transformation into a calm, smiling girl during and after her interaction with McDougall.

Mac's message was clear—
"These frail children are dear!"
With his strong healing ways
(He deserved endless praise),
He was moved to soothe
  kids, far and near.

Some felt heat
High up on their seat—
Others saw colorful rays.
All knew
That this was due
To Old Mac's Magical Ways!

As McDougall worked with the children, they usually reacted in some way. Some would sweat and turn beet red. Some would scratch their heads. Others would relax and fall forward, even falling asleep.

For seven years McDougall worked alone. Finally, it became apparent that he had transferred his healing capacities to one of the other horses, Sere, and then others followed. As a master teacher and a master healer, Mac created a profound equine healing experience for children at Serendipity Stables.

Master Mac

Sere

Mac's healing magic was so great,
He knew, before it got too late,
His horse friends must learn it, too.
So he taught them what to do—
And healing then became their fate.

Yankee

*Sere and others learned watching Mac.
Yankee came later, and to keep him on track,
Mac stood with him—for a month nose to nose.
So when Mac's time came to a close,
He had passed healing magic to Yankee and that's that.*

Magical Mac

As the oldest living horse,
Old McDougall trod a true course.
Having lived a full fifty,
He sure was nifty,
Always a loving and healing bright force.

In 1996, when Mac was 48 years old, a Purina Feed representative called Michele to say, "Do you know that the oldest living horse in America is living with you?" And so he was!

On Mac's 50th, a hundred friends came,
To honor the old horse's great fame.
They gave him a party and gifts galore,
A cake made from his favorite treats—and much more.
Old Mac was tired, but gracious just the same.

Old Mac's favorites: apples, oranges, pears, watermelon, carrots and peppermint candy

MacDougall always lived with force,
Far beyond life's usual course.
That is why his stories we tell
(Those of us who knew him well):
To remember Magical Mac,
  the great healing horse.

This certificate certifies that Mac was the only horse to receive the "Companionship Award."

This medallion was awarded to Mac as he was inducted into the Animal Hall of Fame.

The American Quarter Horse Association and Purina conducted the research that led them to declare Mac the "Oldest Living Horse in America."

The Ohio House of Representatives paid homage to Mac's unselfish ability to enhance the lives of children.

By the time he was 50 years old, McDougall was named to the Animal Hall of Fame and received awards from both Purina and the Ohio House of Representatives. He was also immortalized in the August 1998 issue of *Reader's Digest*, in Annette Foglino's article, "Some Sort of Magic."

The Tail End

About Magical Mac
By Michele S. Davis, Ph.D.

"You will be riding Skunk today," was the statement that set in motion a process we continue to celebrate. I stood transfixed before the Sylvan Stables stall whose wooden nametag gave unmistakable evidence that "Skunk resides here." This first encounter with the equine individual I later renamed McDougall is as clear now as it was twenty-three years ago. Before me stood a massive, seventeen-hands-tall gelding with four white stockings and a white tail. As I beheld this unusual being, he lowered his head, his eyes took on a glazed appearance, and his nostrils flared as his respiration intensified. This majestic healer forewarned me as best he could. I remember commenting to the person at the next stall, "This horse is meditating!"

I don't remember much about that first lesson in August of 1978, but McDougall's honesty, steadiness and talent were both comforting and appealing. Hence, I not only rode him as a lesson horse, but also leased him for several months. (This meant that I paid a percentage of his board at Sylvan Stables and this entitled me to three rides a week outside of lesson time.)

Then, in September 1979, I heard the rumor that McDougall was for sale. Astounded that the stable owner, Dee Ladou, would sell such a fine fellow, I inquired, "Why would you consider getting rid of such a competent school horse?" Her answer surprised me: "I am looking for a good retirement home for him." This comment did not deter me from making the proper financial arrangements to transfer McDougall from the lesson-horse side of the barn to the area reserved for privately owned equines.

In November of that same year, McDougall moved to my newly purchased farm in Raymond, Ohio. Shortly thereafter, a local woman stopped in to introduce herself and to comment, "I used to ride a horse that looked just like yours in riding school fifteen years ago and his name was Skunk. He was about fifteen years old at the time!" This was only the beginning—no matter where I went someone knew McDougall: a clerk at the local department store, an Ohio State University administrator, a Spanish student at Columbus State Community College. It soon became apparent that I had joined forces with an aged equine. So his nickname underwent a modification—from "Big Mac" to "Old Mac."

In order to focus the old fellow on retirement, relaxation and fun, we gave up jumping and dressage in favor of parades and trail rides. Due to his size, his unusual coloration and his dignified presence, McDougall was a favorite in all the local community parades. On several occasions he was even called upon to lead the processions.

As Old Mac entered his mid-to-late thirties, I began getting calls from parents who wanted their autistic children to interact with a gentle and safe horse. At that time, Old Mac's companion, Sully's Southern Rebel, known as Sammy, was in her late twenties. Therefore I offered the use of both Mac and Sam for the enhancement of these special children. Interestingly, the elderly mare showed no interest in these youngsters. However, the aged giant of a gelding was overjoyed to see and serve the needy tykes who lay or sat on his back.

In fact, as Mac's first little visitor lay still and stiff, I saw an astounding repeat of our first meeting. Mac lowered his head, his eyes took on a glazed faraway look, and his nostrils flared as his respiration intensified. While I observed the change in the horse's demeanor, the parents noticed subtle changes in their child's posture. To everyone's amazement the formerly immobile and inarticulate youngster was attempting to pet the horse's neck. Most amazing of all were the child's attempts to verbalize to Old Mac. In short, this aged equine healer was enhancing his newfound friend in ways that seemed almost incomprehensible to all of us. This youngster visited McDougall regularly for several months and each session on the horse resulted in more and more responsiveness. News of an elderly horse who had a healing effect on ailing children gradually radiated throughout the United States. Numerous families found their way to Ohio searching for the help that McDougall seemed able to impart.

Then, in his forty-eighth year, Old Mac's dedication to these young children received a blessing and a boost, when Purina Horse Feed Company formally declared him to be the "Oldest Living Horse in America." The ripple caused by this announcement brought a flurry of media attention and more frail children to Mac's barn in York Center, Ohio. An old horse's dignity and devotion were again emphasized in a sensitive and tender article entitled "Some Sort of Magic," written by Annette Foglino for the August 1998 issue of *Reader's Digest*.

Shortly thereafter, McDougall made his quiet transition to the "higher life" in his sleep. However, before he moved on, this amazing equine healer transferred his knowledge to his barn mates, Yankee and Sere. Therefore his work continues at Serendipity Stables in York Center, Ohio.

In order to further honor and expand McDougall's influence, Serendipity Stables is currently offering three special events: private session with a healing horse, a free "Wellness Service" every second Sunday of the month for those who want to come to interact with the healing horses, and "Higher Awareness Horses" workshops most Saturdays. For the workshop, the following team will round out the concepts which McDougall embodied: Michele S. Davis, Ph.D., learning specialist and owner of Serendipity Stables; Peg Whitmer, L.M.T., equine massage; Morgen Espe, animal communicator and energy worker; Kriston M. Sherman, D.V.M., A.P.P., certified veterinary Acupuncturist; Alexandra Makris, M.A., animal advocate/author.

For more information, call (937) 358-2190 or write to Michele Davis, 21721 SR 47, West Mansfield, Ohio 43358, or visit our website at http://magicalmac.com

The Magic Goes On

By Alexandra Makris, M.A.

Serendipity Stables looks like and is, on the surface, a very ordinary farm, so I did not expect the extraordinary surprise that I received the first time I went there. It was lunchtime when I arrived and the horses were in the barn about to be fed. As I approached the fenced-in meadow by the barn, I heard someone shout, "The horses are out!" (Horses do not usually leave a barn when it is time to eat!) Then I saw them—running and rolling and romping in the grass. It seemed as if they came out to welcome me! Suddenly, I was moved to tears, overcome by the feeling of familiarity and peace with everything there—not just with the animals, but the ground, the vegetation, the structures, the sky, and the very atmosphere. I had entered into the magical sphere that a beloved old horse named McDougall had created by his life of contemplation and real giving.

This is how I came to that magical place:

When I first heard about Michele and her healing horses, I had been a student of spiritual life for several years. As a result, it seemed that I was becoming sensitive to all living beings. Not that I wanted to, it was just happening. My previous attitude, as an adult, toward animals and other non-human beings had been indifference. But I was immediately interested in speaking with Michele to discover if her horses were, in fact, engaged in healing work. If they were, I thought, these horses could be indicators of the vast potential inherent in all nonhumans for goodness. Perhaps we (humans) are living at the tip of the iceberg, but the biggest part of the iceberg (non-humans) is "below" us, often unseen (ignored) and even unknown (forgotten). We are far from alone in this earthly existence—physically, mentally, and spiritually.

When we met, Michele told me that her stable of healing horses started with her old horse Mac when he began having a healing influence on children in need. Mac would go into a meditative state when the children were placed on his back and things would happen that led to healings of all kinds. This went on for a number of years. Then Michele's other horses began to follow in Mac's hoof prints, so to speak, and now they, too, are healers. Remarkably, even the new horses Michele brings to her farm also begin to work as healers.

I understood then that this healing work involved profound energy. What else could it be? Mac never gave anyone a pharmaceutical prescription, or a psychological session or even a good massage. And the results of Mac's work were more than Band-Aid healing because radical changes were apparent in the health and disposition of those who responded to him.

As it was, I had just been studying about non-humans of all kinds, via the Wisdom-Teaching of Adi Da Samraj. He acknowledges the ability of non-humans to enter readily, by choice, into a state of meditation or contemplation, thereby forgetting their bodies, minds and environment in the infinite depth of being. Could it be that Mac, and now the other horses, in their simplicity and naturally occurring meditations, were able to tap into that depth and transmit it—even intentionally? This is one way to describe something magical that is apparently beyond description and yet is happening.

I began to feel, too, that perhaps the four-legged world is not so different from the two-legged, at the core. If we have our healers, teachers and leaders—even great ones—perhaps the non-humans have theirs. Certainly Mac demonstrated all of the qualities of leadership, teaching and healing, far beyond what we would ordinarily expect from a horse!

I had also, in my studies, learned that if animals are allowed an environment in which to live naturally, they can do what they do—their magic. That seemed to be the way it was in times past when animals were understood to be magical communicators. In modern times this does not seem to be a reality for most people. I wondered then, what if we were to allow a cooperative alliance with the non-human world in this way? How could we help each other? What would they teach us?

There was definitely something going on at Michele's farm that was conducive to this magic. She had, by her own dedication and openness, created a safe and nurturing place of loving care for Mac and all of her animals. Through their alliance, Michele and Mac have created a healing legacy for the horses that live at Serendipity Stables and for all who visit. This is the magic that I felt there, too.

So now that I have found out about Magical Mac and fallen in love with him (haven't you?), there will be more true tales to tell of Mac and his friends. The magic goes on!

The McDougall Dictionary

Here are some words and phrases from the story of Magical Mac that may be new to you. Besides explaining the words, sentences correctly using them are included. Make up your own sentences using the new words. Send pictures that you draw to our mailing address. You can send your sentences and/or any questions or comments to:

Mac's website at http://magicalmac.com or to: Serendipity Stables, 21721 SR 47, West Mansfield, Ohio 43358.

autistic — *someone who does not relate to daily activities (such as speaking, making eye contact, listening).* The autistic child does not play like other kids.

balm — *something that feels soothing.* Hand cream is a nice balm.

belied — *to prove false.* Her smile belied her statement that she was sad.

bred — *selecting parents to create certain qualities in their young.* Racehorses are bred for speed.

capacities — *abilities.* She has the capacities to become a fine artist.

constitution — *the way in which one is made up.* Who do you know with a strong constitution?

determined — *having made one's mind up.* She was determined to learn to swim.

equine — *has to do with horses.* The equine event was exciting.

enthusiasm — *with lots of interest and energy.* What do you do with enthusiasm?

fate — *future.* No one knows his or her fate.

galore — *plentiful.* There are words galore here.

gracious — *having or showing kindness.* Mac was known for being gracious.

gelding — *a male horse that has been neutered.* A gelding cannot father a foal (baby horse).

grizzled — *graying that comes with old age.* The 14-year-old dog was grizzled.

hack — *a run-down horse.* She restored the old hack to health.

hands — *used as a way to measure horses (one hand is about 4 inches).* McDougall was 17 hands tall from the bottom of his hoof to the top of his shoulder.

healer — *one who helps to restore health;*
healing — *restoring to health.* Mac was a healer who helped in the healing of many children.

hearty and hale — *words that mean someone has good health and energy.* The baseball player was hearty and hale.

homage — *to pay respect to by action.* He gave homage to his teacher by giving her his attention.

House of Representatives — *people elected to meet together to make laws.* Ohio and every other state in the USA has a House of Representatives.

hyperactive — *difficulty being calm and giving attention with the whole body.* Taking big, deep breaths may calm hyperactive kids.

immense — *great, huge.* Redwoods are immense trees.

immortalize — *to be remembered forever.* Has the reading of this book immortalized Mac for you?

inducted — *to be formally placed in an offical position.* Being inducted into the Hall of Fame is an honor.

inspired — *filled with great motivation.* He was inspired to learn how to read.

interact — *time spent with another, giving and receiving.* Do you interact with your friends on the playground?

legacy — *anything handed down from someone who was here first.* Mac's legacy was a place of healing.

nifty — *attractive, "cool."* You are wearing a nifty shirt!

profound — *deeply or strongly felt, not just on the surface.* Reading about McDougall has a profound effect on most people.

representative — *one who acts and speaks for others.* He was a representative for the USA at the Olympics.

reputation — *how others view a person, thing or action.* Mac's kind acts earned him a good reputation.

saddlebred — *a mix of Pacers, Thoroughbred, Morgan and Draft horses known for giving an easy ride.* Mac's mother was a saddlebred horse.

serendipity — *easily coming upon lucky or happy discoveries accidentally.* It was such a feeling of serendipity to find a field full of fireflies.

tack — *a course of action; any horse equipment.* A tack room is a good place to store saddles.

thoroughbred — *any breed of racehorse bred from the original mix of English with Turkish and Arabic horses.* Mac's father was a thoroughbred horse.

to tend — *to take care of.* The hen knows how to tend her chicks.

traditional — *commonly accepted, usual.* Old Mac's magical ways are not traditional.

transformation — *a change from one way of being or looking to another.* A caterpillar goes through a transformation to become a butterfly.